PRAYER

All royalties from sales of this book will go to Kids Company, working to provide practical, emotional and educational support to vulnerable inner-city children and young people.

www.kidsco.org.uk

PRAYER

Michael Mayne

Introduction by
Joel W. Huffstetler

Foreword by
Brother Patrick Moore

DARTON·LONGMAN + TODD

This edition first published in 2013 by
Darton, Longman and Todd Ltd
1 Spencer Court
140 – 142 Wandsworth High Street
London SW18 4JJ

Previously published in hardback in 2011.

ISBN: 978-0-232-53016-2

A catalogue record for this book is available from the
British Library

Phototypeset by Kerrypress Ltd, Luton, Bedfordshire.
Printed and bound in Great Britain by Bell & Bain,
Glasgow.

Contents

❧

Foreword

These last few years there seems to have been a proliferation of books on prayer. However, this one by Michael Mayne is, I think, unique. This reads more like a conversation with a wise and well-read friend rather than a book of instruction. He is walking along with the reader rather than dispensing directions. The people who participated in the Day of Prayer at Westminster Abbey when he first gave these talks were fortunate, but so are we who are able to follow his thought in this second edition of *Prayer*.

Although each of us have our favourite ways of praying which may have been helpful for us in the past, Michael's concentration is on that contemplation which is the loving attention – that gaze on the divine – which places him in that long tradition which stretches from Augustine to Thomas Merton. Our guide rightly refers to Gregory the Great in reminding us that this loving contemplative gaze is not something reserved for a few chosen souls but open to all. In the words of Gregory the Great, 'Anyone who *keeps his heart within* (what a striking phrase) may be illumined by the light of contemplation'.

As in his other marvellous books Michael directs the reader to other writers such as William Temple, W. B. Yeats, Meister Eckhart, Monica Furlong and Dennis Potter. But these pages are not an historical survey but the telling of an unfolding story which has resonance in the contemporary society where so many of us are searching for that reconnection with the divine (which is certainly the original meaning of the word 'religion').

Michael helps the reader by sharing his own experience in prayer, especially when speaking of how the words of the song known as Saint Patrick's Breastplate lead to a personal encounter with Christ through a moving meditation on the phrases of this ancient hymn. The centrality of Christ in this small book is a theme to which he frequently returns.

For me the strongest element in this little book is Michael's initial invitation to the reader to reflect on his or her personal image of God. He sees that this probably determines not only how we pray but whether we pray at all. He refers to William Temple's insight when he wrote, 'If you have a false idea of God then the more religious you are the worse it is for you, for it were better to be an atheist'. If our prayer is not a response to the call of the One who initiates the entire process then there is little profit. This book gently leads the reader to respond to the Lover who makes the first move in this encounter with the divine.

Patrick Moore
De La Salle Brother and
Scholar-in-Residence at Sarum College

Introduction

Westminster Abbey, situated in the heart of London mere steps away from the Houses of Parliament and 10 Downing Street, is one of the major tourist destinations in the world, drawing over a million visitors a year. Many of the Abbey's guests come strictly as tourists, with no overtly spiritual interest in the Abbey as a functioning church.

When Michael Mayne assumed the deanship of the Abbey in 1986 one of his chief aims was to make the Abbey more obviously a place of prayer. For Mayne, prayer was to be the very lifeblood of the Abbey's daily life and ministry. Friends and colleagues of Mayne (d. 2006) universally remember him as a person of prayer, and during his ten years as overseer of one of Britain's great national shrines Mayne remained true to his pastoral instincts and was keen to ensure that the Abbey's very heartbeat be that of prayer.

In his third year as Dean, Mayne proposed that once a year, on a Saturday, the Abbey should be closed to all visitors and tourists and that an ecumenical Day of Prayer should be held – a day of teaching and learning, a day of theory and practice, thereby affirming the Abbey's primary function as a church, and encouraging people to explore together the life of prayer, which Mayne regarded as the spiritual practice that is at once the most natural and the most difficult. The first such Day of Prayer was held in 1989 with hundreds in attendance. During Mayne's tenure at the Abbey leaders of the Day of Prayer included the likes of Gerard Hughes, Pia Buxton, Jean Vanier, Sheila Cassidy, Anthony Bloom and Rowan Williams. In the year of his retirement, 1996, Mayne himself was encouraged to lead the day of prayer. His series of talks on this most important of subjects are presented in this volume.

Michael Mayne believed that prayer is not an escape from life, not a ten or fifteen minute 'break' during the day. Rather, prayer is meant to be a regular, disciplined reminder that all of life is to be lived in the awareness of the presence of God. Mayne understood that, for Westerners, in an increasingly fast-paced culture a constant temptation is to let prayer slip, and, when we do make time for prayer, to pray narrowly and self-centredly for one's own needs and wants. *Prayer* contains Michael Mayne's modest, accessible and deeply pastoral guidance as to how one can have prayer be the very foundation of a life lived in the conscious awareness of God's presence and love. Mayne understood that we each have to pray in the way that most appeals to us and comes most naturally, and that at different stages we may need to pray differently.

Michael Mayne's five major books are classics of Anglican spirituality. All remain in print and continue to offer pastoral wisdom and support to readers the world over. In 2010, a collection of Mayne's previously unpublished sermons and addresses was published to a warm reception by grateful readers who recognise Mayne as one of the finest spiritual writers of his generation. With the appearance of *Prayer* we now have Michael Mayne's definitive reflections on prayer widely available for the first time. These addresses are as fresh and as relevant today as they were on that Saturday in 1996 when first delivered. With the advent of this volume on prayer, Michael Mayne has given us yet another classic.

Joel W. Huffstetler
Rector, St Luke's Episcopal Church
Cleveland, Tennessee

1.

In my rather strange childhood the cinema played a central place, and I used to love those Hollywood fantasies in which the chorus girl is suddenly called upon to play the star, or the third attendant finds himself playing Hamlet. In each case the ugly duckling is transformed overnight into a swan. And so today, after eight years in a minor supportive role for this Day of Prayer I am suddenly centre stage and not a little daunted, for I know that by the end of the day I shall remain a rather elderly ugly duckling. However, I know too that the best advice for any speaker is: 'Never apologise in advance, for if you do you demoralise your audience.'

So I won't. I shall assume that we all find prayer extremely difficult, sometimes boring, often baffling. We read this or that spiritual book of advice, as if to become an expert in prayer were as straightforward as to become an expert cook, but somehow the spiritual recipes that look so simple and easy may well not work for me; what Delia swears is foolproof proves to be nothing of the kind: the soufflé fails to rise. In the words of Claudius, uncle to Prince Hamlet:

> *My words fly up, my thoughts remain*
> * below:*
> *Words without thoughts never to heaven*
> * go.*

And that leaves me feeling puzzled, or guilty, or angry. And therefore I want to speak as simply and personally as I can, without making any assumptions about where any of you may be in your own journey to God. Many of you are no doubt ahead of me on the journey. If I seem to you to labour all-too-familiar truths, then be patient for the sake of those who may be hearing those truths for the first time; if my words are tiresomely predictable, then ask yourself if some of the basic building-blocks that you know with your *mind* you know equally in your *heart*, that you feel the truth of them on your pulse and in your very life blood, so that they have become part of your very being.

One truth is plain: we should not be here at all, seeking to love God better, unless we had in some way been grasped *by* him. Unless he were already within our hearts and minds, having planted in us an intuitive desire to explore and become intimate with the very source of our being. Sometimes you are lucky enough to meet those who have spent a lifetime in the quest for God (or, as they might prefer to put it, this journey *into* God). Often it is a religious, a monk or a nun, and their faces are so unmistakably beautiful that you are compelled to ask, not so much 'What have you been doing all these years? What is the secret of your technique?', but 'Who have you been with all this time, for he is so beautiful.'

Henri de Tourville once wrote: 'Say to yourself, "I am loved by God more than I can either conceive or understand." Let this fill all your soul and all your prayers and never leave you. You will soon see that this is the way to find God.' And my prayer is that each of you may catch a new glimpse of the unimaginable fullness and richness of God's love for you: that there will be something in what I say or in how you respond, or what may happen in the silence, that helps you to see or challenges you afresh. Hold on to anything that is life-giving for you and forget the rest. For this is not about me or my words, but about what God will say to you. Will you have become, in some infinitesimal way, a tiny bit more human, more your true self, more what Love is calling you to be? And if only one thing touches you, hold on to it and make it your own.

Our understanding of God

If prayer is the expression of our faith in God, if it is an expression of our desire for the coming of his rule in this deeply troubled world, and of our love for him and his created world of infinitely wonderful people and things, then *how* we pray, and indeed *whether* we pray, depends first and last on our understanding of God. 'If you have a false idea of God', wrote William Temple, 'then the more religious you are the worse it is for you, for it were better to be an atheist.'

So who is the inconceivably powerful Creator who sings the creation into being, and holds it in being moment by moment? In crude terms: Will the real God stand up? Well: yes and no. For if anyone ever gives you a clear and precise notion of who God is, you may be sure it is false. God is mystery, not to be contained in human language or domesticated by human concepts. In St Paul's words: 'How unsearchable his judgements, how untraceable his ways!' And Richard Rolle, writing in the fourteenth century, says this: 'If thou wilt know properly to speak what God is, I fear thou shalt never find an answer to this question … If thou desirest to know what God is, thou desirest to be God … It is enough for thee to know *that God is*.' God is Being, not *a* being, but Being with a capital 'B', the ground of *our* being who moment by moment *gives us* life. Those rare souls who in every age speak of encounters which for them touch on the very heart of reality we call mystics. They claim that the world of matter is pervaded by, and only finds its explanation in, the transcendent reality we call God. And by 'transcendent' they mean that which transcends the bounds of what we can see or hear or touch, that which is both beyond and within, different from and other than, the familiar world of people and things, and yet something to which these seem to point as both their source and their goal. A beyondness which tells of another world.

Awareness of the transcendent and the numinous is what those who belong to what we (rather patronisingly) call 'primitive cultures' know in their bones. It is knowing with a deep undeniable instinctive knowledge that in the depth of myself, in stillness, I am aware of the 'other' that is not me, and yet is the very ground of my existence. And I believe it is precisely this intuitive sense of the transcendent, the muffled presence of the holy, that makes me human.

I use the phrase 'in the depth of myself', and it's interesting how many of the discoveries of twentieth-century psychology bear out the beliefs of so many spiritual teachers in both the East and West that I am a kind of double person. I am conscious of myself in terms of my ego, that ego which is so clamorous, so demanding, that it can deceive me into thinking that it is all that I am. But this is not so, for there is another self, an inner, eternal self, my spirit, that spark of divinity which links me to the Divine Ground; and it is the purpose of my life to discover this true self, until outer and inner reality are one and I achieve an integrity whose marks will be an inner stillness, unity and peace of mind.

So Meister Eckhart, that remarkable thirteenth-century Dominican friar and mystic, wrote of how it is necessary, if we are to be persons in the fullest sense, to become aware of 'a transcendent abyss' within ourselves. He spoke of God as having an infinite capacity for giving, and each human soul an infinite capacity for receiving. He wrote of how each one of us must discover our capacity, little by little, to detach ourselves from this all-demanding ego, and begin to reflect that which is of God that lies at our very centre. For the deepest mystery about you and me is that we can find God in the depths of ourselves, and having begun to do so we can then begin to find him everywhere.

Of course, if that was the whole story, if God was utterly mysterious and other, his life somehow within us and yet still 'the unknown God' of the Athenians, we should not be here today. For even though God would not be God if he could be fully known to us, neither would he be God if he couldn't be known at all. And known in two ways. Known because his Being penetrates the universe. He is a God who uses the language of matter. A God to whom all created things point as the source of their being, each in its unique and particular presence. A God who is sensed in the depths of our being because (to use the rich phrase of Genesis) we are created in his image.

But that is not the half of it. For we believe that this hidden, awesome, reticent God once revealed himself in the only language we can understand: our own. Not in order to answer our perplexed questions but to enter into them with us: living our life and sharing our death. We believe that Jesus who is the Christ, alone of all our race, looked full at the transcendent mystery and said that his name was 'Abba' – Father – and that love was his meaning. Meister Eckhart writes in one of his sermons:

> *There was once a rich man and a rich lady. The lady had an accident and lost one eye, at which she grieved exceedingly. Then the Lord came to her and said, 'Wife, why are you so distressed? You should not be so distressed at losing your eye.' She said, 'Sir, I do not mourn because I have lost my eye, I mourn for the fear you might love me less.' Then he said, 'Lady, I love you.' Not long afterwards he put out one of his own eyes, and going to his wife, he said, 'Lady, so you may know that I love you I have made myself like you; now I too have only one eye.' This is like man, who could scarcely*

believe that God loved him so much, until
God put out one of his own eyes and
assumed human nature.

This is an extraordinary claim. It means that from the moment of the Big Bang some 15 billion years ago – through the gradual evolution over thousands of millions of years of the material universe, then of life, then of consciousness, through the man who spoke of God as Abba, through the words of St Augustine's confessions and the music of Beethoven's last quartets, and the language of Lear and Othello – the Love who, in Dante's words, 'moves the sun and the other stars' was fulfilling one purpose – the deepest possible happiness of those made in his likeness. It means that all this was implicit from the beginning of creation.

And that is the *real* God, the authentic God, to whom we are invited to respond. And prayer begins with a simple, contemplative awareness of God as Being, God as Christlike, and of yourself as one who is grasped and held and loved and invited to respond; an awareness of that loving relationship. 'Our whole business in life',

wrote St Augustine, 'is to restore to health the
eye and the heart whereby God may be seen.'

Our understanding of ourselves

I began with a question: 'Will the real God stand up?' The answer is that the real God is pure unbounded love, shown to be so in a series of images or icons: a blind man restored to sight, a guilty woman forgiven, the washing of dusty feet, the breaking of bread with friends, the body hanging on a cross. This disclosure both crowns and corrects whatever else may have been said about God and his relationship with his world. But it leads us to another question: 'Will the real *me* please stand up?' For each of us is a kind of double person on a double journey. The outer journey, the public journey, has to do with people and places and events, with doing and achieving. The inner, private journey has to do with a different kind of exploration, and it needs different words with which to describe it: words like faith and trust and wonder. Words like penitence and forgiveness and self-giving love. Words which have to do with that giving attention to God and to his world and to people that is the nerve centre of all religious belief and practice.

I believe that it is as we exercise our faculty of wonder, of giving proper attention, that we become aware of the beyond in our midst. One of our most God-like characteristics is to learn how to *be*, for there is a still centre at the very deepest part of us where we are ourselves without subtraction. But it is a sacred place, and sacred places are a bit scary. Hugh Lavery has written:

> *We are citizens of two worlds. The temporal is the world of work and worry, the world that is too much with us. But we have other experiences, brief ecstasies, still moments when we enter the Kingdom. Then we cease to do. We simply are. Being silences and subdues doing and the temporal melts into the eternal.*

So, that aspect of giving attention that we call prayer is something I do, not primarily to *achieve* anything, but just because this is the *sort* of creature I am. I know I am dust, that one day my body will return to the earth, that I am finite and limited, self-centred and sinful; but I know equally that I am capable of giving myself in love to others and taking delight in receiving love from them. I am dust that dreams of a different destiny, for I know that I am a 'lover-in-the-making', and that the surest way to my true destiny is to reflect upon, give my attention to, and respond to, the one whose nature and whose name is Love. We have a natural desire to respond to beauty and truth and goodness, a natural sense of thankfulness when we are pleased or happy or in love, a natural desire to feel we are loved when we are sad or in pain or grieving, a natural sense of shame when we have caused hurt to others. Which is why 'I love you' and 'thank you' and 'I trust you' and 'I am sorry' are the basic ingredients of our prayer life.

Now to grow in true selfhood must mean growing in relationship with others in the give and take of love. Yet that doesn't mean losing my own unique selfhood. This seems to me so important a truth, for it touches deeply both on how I value myself and also how I understand my relationship with God.

God the creator of the universe does not go in for mass production: I am specially designed, made in his likeness, and there is a special place in his providence that only I can fill. In the psalmist's words:

> *I will give thanks unto thee, for I am fearfully and wonderfully made ... Thou hast fashioned me behind and before: and laid thine hand upon me. Thine eyes did see my substance, yet being unperfect: and in thy book were all my members written.*

I have a unique responsibility: one that can't be delegated to anyone else. Moreover, my capacity to respond to God and to love him is unique to me. He has made me for this, and he desires to draw me to him. I may be a sinful, neglectful, moody, unloving and very complex human being; but the truth I need to learn and re-learn and learn again until it is as natural to me as breathing is that I am also the uniquely valued, uniquely loved, child of God: redeemed and accepted and forgiven. And loved not in *spite* of being me, but because I *am* me. That, believe it or not, *is* the gospel. Only a few days ago I had a letter from a woman, a priest's wife, in which she said: 'I've spent most of my life unlearning the disapproving God.'

But what of this 'self', this innermost soul, that lies so deep within me and that is something much more than that 'ego' that so clamours for attention? In his jewel-like essay *On the Love of God* St Bernard writes of four degrees of love: the first is the love of self; the second is the love of God for what he gives, which is still a selfish love; the third is the love of God for what he is. But it's the fourth and final degree of love, not to be attained by most of us in this life, that is the interesting one: for the final kind of love, says St Bernard, is *love of self and neighbour for God's sake.* Thomas Merton comments on those words:

> *These words show that the fulfilment of our destiny is not merely to be lost in God … like a 'drop of water in a barrel of wine or like iron in the fire' but found in God in all our individual and personal reality, tasting our eternal happiness … in*

> *the fact that we can see his will done in us
> at last.*

Note those words: they matter. We shall find our eternal happiness 'in finally allowing God's will to be done in us *in all our individual and personal reality'*. Just as in human terms my relationship with those I love is mine and mine alone, so it is with God. What makes me and every other living soul of unique and irreplaceable value in God's sight is that I have my own special identity that can never be replicated. It isn't that I am special because I have particular gifts and talents. I am special (as you are special) because we each have a personal, intimate relationship with God which is ours and ours alone, and it is this that makes us precious in his sight.

The poet W. B. Yeats once wrote of one of those small epiphanies – those moments of clear perception – that come just occasionally into our lives, when we suddenly see some truth afresh. 'I was walking one day', he writes,

> *over the bit of marshy ground close to Inchy
> Wood when there swept over me a sense of
> dependence on a great personal Being some-*

where far off yet near at hand, and I heard a
voice speaking to me saying, 'No human soul is
like any other human soul, and therefore the
love of God for any human soul is infinite, for
no other soul can satisfy the same need in God.'

Our growth in the image and likeness of God, as
we see that likeness in Jesus Christ, is the exact
opposite of some Buddhist denial of the reality of
this entity called 'me', the extinction of the self
that Nirvana brings. On the contrary. It means
discovering at last what it really means to be *me*,
when I am opened at last to God's transforming
and affirming Spirit. It is like a relationship of a
good marriage or a deep friendship, when the
more you give yourself away in the give and take
of love the more your true self is discovered and
affirmed. Those who wish to gain their lives must
be prepared to lose them. If I seem to labour this
point it is because I believe that only as we
understand God's need of me as well as my need
of God, does my prayer become a grateful and
loving response to a given relationship.

Prayer: who we are and whose we are

Prayer, then, is not primarily something *one does*, but something *that is*. We accept as a matter of faith that it is in God that we live and move and have our being, that his life and spirit are always in us waiting to be released into expression. 'Though God be everywhere present', wrote William Law in the eighteenth century, 'yet he is present to thee in the deepest and most central part of the soul.' That is the primary, given reality: the relationship out of which we cannot fall, and all our little acts of prayer, our vocal prayers, our times of meditation or that prayer of loving attention that we call contemplation – all these are secondary: conscious and disciplined reminders of who we are and whose we are. For prayer is not an escape from life, not ten or fifteen or twenty minutes cut out of my life, nor a relationship to be forged afresh every time, but a regular, disciplined reminder that all life is lived in the presence of God. It's like a marriage relationship, not a flirtation carried out in a series of clandestine meetings. Prayer is marvelling at God's love as that is shown in Christ, and receiving and responding to that transcendent reality by whom we have been grasped, and whom we sense at our very centre.

You will remember St Augustine's words:

> *Too late have I loved thee, O thou beauty of ancient days, yet ever new! Too late have I loved thee! And behold, thou wert within, and I abroad. Thou wert with me, but I was not with Thee.*

Commenting on Augustine's words a century ago, Bishop Ullathorne wrote:

> *Let it be understood that we cannot turn to God unless we first enter into ourselves … God is everywhere but not everywhere to us; and there is one point in the universe*

where God connects with us and that is the
centre of our own soul. There he waits for
us: there he meets us. To see him we enter
our own interior.

And St Teresa, in writing about St Augustine's
words, adds:

We are not forced to take wings to find
God, but have only to seek solitude and to
look within ourselves. You need not be
overwhelmed with confusion before so kind
a Guest, but with utter humility, talk to
him as to your Father: ask for what you
want as from your father: tell him your
sorrows and beg him for relief.

Seek solitude and look within yourself

You may be thinking: 'What about the nuts and bolts of prayer? Let's get down to the practical nitty gritty.' Later in the book, I will write about the importance of giving attention, about the relation of public and private prayer, and say a bit about intercession, about silence and posture and motivation. But, before that, let me remind you of the basic forms of prayer: and then suggest a practical exercise that you might like to try.

There are three different ways of prayer. You can use words in which to speak to God; you can use a passage of scripture or some spiritual book as a basis for meditation, using your mind and imagination; or you can use silence, just being still before God in the prayer of loving attention.

And we each have to learn to pray in the way that attracts us, the way that comes most *naturally*; though we may find that we shift a little at different stages of our life.

Let me speak of my times of prayer in very personal terms, of what it's like for me. (I am not speaking now of the daily Offices or the Liturgy.) I have to say that I have never found mental prayer very easy. I am not a push-over for the Ignatian method of meditation: Ignatius of Loyola, as many of you know, based his spiritual exercises on a carefully graded series of gospel stories, the imaginative meditation and contemplation of a parable, a healing miracle, or the words of Jesus. Many find the discipline of these exercises a very potent way of growing in their faith and allowing their hidden self to grow strong, and I suppose the growth of Ignatian-style retreats and one-to-one counselling have been the most significant advance in people's spiritual lives in a very long while.

I find I need something simpler, something that makes less of a mental demand. I am happier with the Sulpician method of prayer that originated in the parish of St Sulpice in Paris in the seventeenth century. This simply involves taking a simple passage from the gospels and considering it in three different ways: Jesus before the eyes – or Christ before you; Jesus in the heart – or Christ within you; Jesus in the hands – or Christ through you. We see Jesus in one aspect of his Godlikeness: we take the meaning into our hearts: we resolve what our response will be. The movement is from eyes to heart and from heart to hands. Christ before me, Christ within me, Christ through me.

But I am happiest of all with that kind of loving attention that is a form of contemplation, sometimes called affective prayer or simple contemplation. I don't think the titles matter. When I was at theological college we were taught that contemplation was a very advanced form of prayer, a form of adoration only given to the select few. I now think that's misleading. St Gregory the Great wrote that 'It is not true that the grace of contemplation is given to the highest and not to the lowest. Anyone who *keeps his heart within* (what a striking phrase!) may be illumined by the light of contemplation.' St Gregory has a kind of signature tune that he repeats over and over again: the phrase 'to keep and return to one's heart or inner self'. Every one of us has within him or her, however much or little we may be aware of it, a contemplative dimension. And Michael Ramsey writes of how simple contemplative prayer is something accessible to what he calls 'even very backward Christians', and he adds:

> *This waiting on God in quietness may be our greatest service to the world if in our very apartness the love for people is on our hearts.*

Contemplation begins and ends with stillness. A stillness of the body, and, much more difficult, of the mind and spirit, learning (as St John of the Cross says) 'to be still in God, fixing our loving attention upon him'. You no longer try to talk or even to think. It's the difference between meeting a stranger or a casual acquaintance and searching for things to say, and being with someone you love who knows you intimately, no longer needing any words because the relationship binds you in a silent and mutual love and trust.

To contemplate is quite literally to give attention: to look, to gaze, to focus on something or someone with one's whole being. When we are caught up in listening to music, or gazing at a work of art, or faced with some wonder of the natural world, or in certain moments of happiness the mind is at rest. It is simply attending in quietness and joy to what is before it. It is this faculty of the mind to attend, without one thought giving way to another, simply to be held, to wait in silence, that is the characteristic feature of contemplation. We are all familiar with it at certain times, and some would say that it is the commonest, wisest, safest way to God.

But we need a focus on which to centre our attention. It may be visual: an icon, a crucifix, a candle, a flower. Or it may be – and for me it almost always is – a word or a familiar phrase, or words known by heart, words that become therefore much more a prayer of the heart than of the mind. That medieval book of instruction called *The Cloud of Unknowing* describes our familiar dilemma of finding we can't keep our attention on God by reflecting on a passage of scripture or a phrase or an object. And the anonymous author tells us to strike out with 'the sharp dart of longing love'. 'Short prayer', he writes, 'penetrates heaven … the shorter the word the better, being more like the working of the Spirit – a word like "God" or "love".' Some will use as a kind of mantra the words 'Abba', or 'Father' – that intimate word for God used uniquely by Jesus; or the Jesus prayer (Lord Jesus Christ, Son of the living God, have mercy on me, a sinner); or a phrase from the Lord's Prayer; or a verse from the psalms, said repeatedly, slowly and rhythmically, until your mind is still. I sometimes use 'Come, Lord Jesus', or the phrase '*This* is the day that the Lord has made: let us rejoice and be glad in it', or 'It is right at all times, and in all places, to give thanks'. I can't recommend too strongly learning one or two prayers or phrases that in a few words contain the heart of the Christian mystery, and which you will go on using and which will serve you all your days, in all times and in all places, the prayer perhaps you would like to be saying when you come to die.

But in saying these words you are trying to enter the stillness, not launching yourself on some mental process. And when distractions come, as they do all the time, it is the repetition of the mantra, the phrase, the name for God, that will bring you back and back again until the mind becomes stilled.

I suppose the words that I have grown to use and love more than any other are words from that ancient hymn called St Patrick's Breastplate. And I want to end by suggesting just a little of their deep meaning. They are the words which begin 'Christ be with me, Christ within me', and I have no doubt they are inspired by St Paul's reference to our life in Christ, which was his own daily experience. 'God's secret plan', he writes, 'now made clear, is simply this: Christ in you.' And again, writing to the Church in Ephesus:

> *May the Father, through his Spirit, enable you to grow firm in power with regard to your inner self, so that Christ may live in your heart through faith, that ... knowing the love of Christ, which is beyond knowledge, you may be filled with the utter fullness of God.*

So-called 'breastplate' hymns were often used as baptism hymns on Easter Eve: and this particular verse from St Patrick's Breastplate – Christ be with me, Christ within me – will have been sung as the response of those to be baptised. 'Let us put on faith and love as a breastplate', St Paul had written, 'let your armour be the Lord Jesus Christ.' And I try to say at the start of each day this comprehensive and strengthening prayer. You can use it to intercede for people, or you can use it to lead you into a time of silent attentiveness.

Christ be with me: Jesus, called Emmanuel, God with us: Jesus the Christ, in whom God uniquely lived and moved and had his being. Who for us reveals that God is Christlike: with us at every moment, asking only that we trust that this is so.

Christ within me: His Spirit, as he promised, acting silently, invisibly at the level of my spirit. Prompting me. Opening my eyes a little to the truth about him, about myself, about others; opening my eyes to the beauty of the natural world but also to human need.

Christ behind me: With me in the past, from the moment the waters of baptism brought me into the Christian family. The one who has changed the direction of my human journey, so that as I look back I see Christ, as it were, giving me a vision and a goal, setting the boundaries of how I should try to live.

Christ before me: Christ in my future. Christ with me to the moment of my death and beyond. In Christ I shall pass through the awesome experience of dying and cannot be separated even by death from the God he reveals.

Christ beside me: Christ a protective presence when I am scared; a consoling presence when I am hurt; a forgiving presence when I am ashamed; a heartening presence when I am discouraged.

Christ to win me: For I am not won yet. Half converted, half trusting, not all that loving. And it is only the love of God, that unimaginable love I glimpse in Christ, that as I come to realise it more and more will prove persuasive in drawing me home to God.

Christ to comfort and restore me: To comfort means 'to make strong', 'to affirm', 'to encourage'. Christ to strengthen me in time of need. Christ to encourage me when I endure hardship or suffer for his sake. Christ to heal, to renew, to make me 'at one' again, both with God and my neighbour. Christ whose love I experience as forgiveness.

Christ beneath me: Christ above me: 'If I go up to heaven thou art there: if I go down to hell thou art there also.' There is no place I can go, no state in which I can be, where I am not in God's presence in Christ. 'Underneath are the everlasting arms.'

Christ in quiet, Christ in danger: Christ in the stillness, where God dwells. Christ when we are alone, when the world's noise and our mental noise is stilled. But with us too wherever danger lurks. Julian of Norwich wrote: 'He said not: Thou shalt not be tested, thou shalt not be travailed, thou shalt not be afflicted: but he said: thou shalt not be overcome.'

Christ in hearts of all who love me: Christ in those to whom I give and from whom I receive love. Christ in his body, the local church of which I am part.

Christ in mouth of friend and stranger: But here is a deeper mystery. The mystery of the Christ present in all who are in need, Christ in what Mother Teresa calls 'the distressing disguise of the poorest of the poor'.

At the Last Supper, Jesus had said to his followers: 'Because I live, you too will live; then you will know that I am in the Father, and you in me and I in you.' And right at the end, he said: 'Be assured, I am with you; yes, to the end of time.' What more could God have done than that which he has done already in Christ to prove to us the nature of his great love, and to invite our response?

2.

I want to return to the question of stillness. For many people the discovery of the value of silence is the most important discovery in their spiritual lives. I don't say the easiest, for sometimes silence is threatening, a bit frightening. Yet it is also the awakening of a thirst that never leaves us: the thirst for that inner stillness in which God is to be found. In the words of the seventeenth-century bishop, Jeremy Taylor: 'There should be in the soul halls of space, avenues of leisure, and high porticos of silence, where God walks.'

'To be passive and receptive', wrote Monica Furlong in 1971, 'is the feminine pole of human experience, and no-one can be creative without it.' She writes of what the Zen masters call a 'purposeless tension' – like the surface tension of a pool of water, or the tension of the string of an instrument waiting to be played. The purpose of striving for such stillness is so we may fix our attention in such a way as to achieve a different state of consciousness: what the Eastern Orthodox tradition describes as 'putting the mind in the heart'. It isn't thinking, it isn't day-dreaming, it isn't really listening. It is a tension which comes from an inner relaxation, a waiting on God, as described in R. S. Thomas's poem *Kneeling.*

'In the beginning was the Word', writes St Augustine, 'this is he to whom Mary listened; and the Word was made flesh, this is he whom Martha served.' And the Christian life is a listening and a serving, a waiting on God and a loving him in his creation, and the serving and the loving are directed aright by the listening and the waiting that is the heart of prayer.

It is a truth born of the concept of God *resting* on the seventh day, actively and lovingly contemplating his finished creation, and it is this loving attention of God that keeps all things in being. So Monica Furlong writes of the natural rhythm of life, a rhythmic quality we can still see in primitive people and in animals, activity alternating with passivity, rather than this endless, anxious, busy-ness that afflicts us all.

Yet achieving it is a different matter. In *The Flight of the Kingfisher*, written after several months living with the Aborigines, Monica Furlong writes:

> *By the quality of their lives the Aborigines showed me something of the failure of my own. I lacked their physicality and, like all of us in our western world, I had suffered a dysfunction from nature which I believe needs a kind of healing I can still only imagine ... Unlike them, I could not sit still, not unless I was 'occupied'. I could not simply commune with myself by myself for hours, and so could never know the special tranquility out of which the deepest kind of understanding is born. To know the lack is, in part, to guess at the wealth the West denies itself. For me, the task is only just begun and it will take me the rest of my life. And if my Christian forebears are to be believed, beyond that.*

'Nothing in all creation is so like God as stillness', wrote Meister Eckhart; and achieving this kind of inner stillness is, I believe, at the heart of what today is about, for it lies at the heart of what the Christian journey is about. It is about learning to see: learning to look at yourself and your neighbour and the world about you with changed eyes, with the inward eye, with what St Paul calls 'the eye of the heart'. And that giving attention to God that we call prayer is about learning to become still, so that we are open and receptive to the 'now', to what Père de Caussade called 'the sacrament of the present moment' in which God alone is to be found. He is here, in *this* moment and no other; this and every moment is the point of intersection between the moment in time and the timeless, eternal moment in which we are held by God. God is the dynamic stillness at the heart of the universe, Eliot's 'still point of the turning world/where the dance is', which is why our hearts seek rest and are restless until they rest in him.

Loving with God's love,
seeing with God's gaze

If all this is true then it turns on its head a common assumption that the most important aspect of prayer is bringing our needs, or the needs of others, to God. For the proper relationship in prayer is that we attend upon God in order to hear what God wills, and we do that by inviting God's dynamic, loving energy, which we call the Holy Spirit, that is at our centre to open our eyes. 'We commonly write about the Holy Spirit', writes Bishop John Taylor,

> *as the source of power. But in fact he enables us not by making us supernaturally strong but by opening our eyes. He opens*

*my eyes to Christ, to the brother and sister
in Christ, or our fellow man or woman, or
the point of need, or the heartbreaking
brutality and the equally heart-breaking
beauty of the world.*

'By virtue of the creation and still more of the
incarnation', writes Teilhard de Chardin, 'nothing here below is profane for those who know
how to see. On the contrary, everything is
sacred.' And there is a lovely quotation from a
book by Max Warren, one-time canon of Westminster, in which he writes: 'Our first task in
approaching another person, another culture,
another religion, is to take off our shoes, for the
place we are approaching is holy. Else we may
find ourselves treading on men's dreams. More
serious still, we may forget that God was here
before our arrival.'

I am reminded of the assertion of another
canon of Westminster, William Temple, that religious experience is not some special, isolated
aspect of human life, but that religious experience is the *whole* experience of a religious person, one who has faith in the ever-present God.
And attentiveness, equally, shouldn't be confined

to certain privileged moments: each object, each person, each happening offers us a wondrous richness if only we will pay attention to what Shakespeare calls 'the mystery of things'. Nothing banal or insignificant. It is we who trivialise and skim the surface of life. Which is I guess what Meister Eckhart meant in saying that '[holiness] consists in doing the next thing you have to do, doing it with your whole heart, and finding delight in doing it.'

If it is true that my prayer is not just about certain moments, specially ringed-off short times cut out of my daily life, but a way of seeing my whole life as containing a significance and beauty it would not otherwise have, what does such contemplative living (and contemplative praying) entail? How do we learn to see with newly-opened eyes?

The person whose work has been such a help to me is the Jewish writer Martin Buber. In his now classic book *I and Thou* he writes that there are two ways of looking at everything. The first is the way of seeing a thing objectively, analysing it as a scientist might, and using it, perhaps even exploiting it. That is what he calls the 'I–It' relationship. The second is the way of contemplation, of empathy, harmony, understanding and love, which is the relationship of 'I–Thou'. In Buber's words, 'All real living is meeting', and again 'if you explore the life of things and hallow it you meet the living God'.

The whole essence of contemplation, and of prayer as contemplation, is empathy, our ability to project our personality into what is in front of us, be it a tree or a human being; or if you are Julian of Norwich, a hazelnut, in which she learned that if you give your attention to the tiniest object, each created in its own small perfection, you find the creative power of God who is both the sustainer and lover of all that exists.

The writer Philip Toynbee, during the last two years in which he was battling with cancer, learned to look at trees as if for the first time:

> *25 October St Luke's summer. Trees have the power to startle me more and more. I seem to be looking at a tree for the first time.*
>
> *19 November Tree scrutiny ... I stand and look; looking I respect, almost to the point of love. But what I hope to be loving is God;*

*not because he 'made' the tree but because
he gives me the power to see it with such
intensity and clarity.*

And a month before he died he writes:

*Wet leaves of may and sycamore after a
heavy shower, and the sun glittering on
them as the wind shakes them. Such things
I now look at with renewed intensity and
happiness – not because I may not see them
for much longer, but because they are of
immediate significance: almost direct
manifestations of heavenly life.*

And do you remember that last amazing televi-
sion interview with Dennis Potter just before he
too died of cancer, when he said:

*We forget that life can only be defined in the
present tense; it is, and it is now … and
that nowness becomes so vivid to me that I
am almost serene. Below my window the
blossom is out in full. And it is the whitest,
frothiest, blossomest blossom there ever
could be. And I can see it; and things are*

both more trivial than they ever were and
more important than they ever were, and
the difference between the trivial and the
important doesn't seem to matter, but the
nowness of everything is absolutely
wondrous.

Now you may think we have moved a long way from the meaning and practice of prayer. But have we? For what I am suggesting is that the more we can learn to achieve stillness, the more we shall learn little by little to give that quality of attention which is a small act of love. Evelyn Underhill once wrote:

The condition of all valid seeing and
hearing … lies in a peculiar attitude of the
whole personality: in a self-forgetting
attentiveness, a profound concentration
which operates a real communion between
the seer and the seen – in a word, in
contemplation.

'Let your soul be in your eyes', she writes; and she advises that we take a simple object such as a leaf, a stone, a candle, a picture, an icon, a flower, a tree, a hillside, running water, our own hand.

She advises us to look at this object and, gently but firmly, allow the distractions with which our mind is filled to drop into the background, focusing simply and wholly on what is before us. She writes:

Do not think, but as it were pour out your personality towards it: let your soul be in your eyes. Almost at once, this new method of perception will reveal unsuspected qualities in the external world. First, you will perceive about you a strange and deepening quietness; a slowing down of our feverish mental time. Next, you will become aware of a heightened significance, an intensified existence in the thing at which you look. As you, with all your consciousness, lean out towards it, an answering current will meet yours. It seems as though the barrier between its life and your own, between subject and object, had melted away. You are merged with it, in an act of true communion: and you know the secret of its being deeply and unforgettably, yet in a way which you can never hope to express.

Only the saint achieves the ability to see all creatures and all created things in the I–Thou rather than the I–It relationship. The rest of us occasionally succeed, but much more often fail. But if we can see the way of prayer that is a form of simple contemplation as a kind of *concentrate* of what life is supposed to be, this empathetic harmony with each other and with all living things will grow in us, as the Holy Spirit gently draws us out of ourselves and into a closer unity with Christ.

Through him, with him, in him

I want to say something about the relation of
private and public prayer. There is, of course, no
such thing as private prayer, a kind of private
telephone line to God. For if we are seeking to
open ourselves to the one God, partaking of one
baptism, and as members of the one body of
Christ, then our times of conscious prayer are
much more like taking up our flutes or our
fiddles and joining in a great symphony of praise
and thanksgiving – one in which the music never
stops, and where to pray is to join in what is
already going on both on earth and in heaven.
Prayer is one of those things which can't be just a
private pursuit even in a culture like ours,
obsessed as it is with privatisation and consumer

choice. Any large bookshop now has a range of do-it-yourself spiritualities. Well, pray as you *can* and *not* as you can't, certainly; and yes, we each have our own unique relationship to God; but this way of perceiving the spiritual life is a thousand miles from that of the New Testament where virtually no interest is shown in the inner life of the individual.

The New Testament is not so much concerned with bringing Jesus into my life as with bringing us into his. It is concerned with the new creation, the new humanity in Christ, the building up of the body of Christ. St Paul is almost obsessed with that crucial phrase 'in Christ', *en Christo*; it is so vital to his thought that it occurs in his letters over 160 times. Most of our Christian praying is done publicly in our public worship, in the liturgy, the Eucharist, the Mass. Private prayer is our attempt to extend this into our daily life rather than the other way round.

The truth is, we remain egos when we set ourselves apart from other egos; we only become *persons* by our willingness to enter into relationship with *other* persons. We talk of society, but the whole concept of society is meaningless unless each of its individual members knows what it means to say 'I am *me*, not you'; but equally you cannot discover what it really means to say 'I am' unless you have also learned what it means to say 'we are'. Indeed, it is in the recognition of other people's uniqueness by seeing them with love that we become aware of God as the mystery who is in and between us, holding us and uniting us at the centre of our beings.

And this is where intercession comes in. 'I am just going to pray for you at St Paul's', wrote Sidney Smith to a friend, 'though with no very lively hope of success.' (He should have tried the Abbey!) In intercession, sincerity is not enough. We can be sincere but entirely selfish. I think of that delightful prayer found among the papers of John Ward MP, who, in the eighteenth century, owned estates in Dagenham:

> O Lord, Thou knowest I have mine estates in the City of London, and likewise that I have lately purchased an estate in fee-simple in the County of Essex. I beseech Thee to preserve the two counties of Middlesex and Essex from fire and earthquake, and, as I have a mortgage in Hertfordshire, I beg of Thee likewise to have an eye of compassion on that county; for the rest of

the counties, Thou mayest deal with them as
Thou art pleased …

But of course intercession is not a way of changing God's mind, but of changing ourselves and, if
God wills it, those for whom we pray. Of course
God *can* run his universe without our help, but
he has chosen not to, and though many things are
God's will – peace and justice for starters – they
will not happen unless and until we actively seek
and work for them. Our lives are bound up at
every level and we are asserting this when we
hold those we love, or those we have hurt or who
have hurt us, or those in need, in God's presence,
saying: 'Lord, we do not presume to tell you what
to do, nor how or when to do it. We simply bring
before you those who need your love, and needs
your grace alone can meet.'

Again I believe that when we pray for others,
our task is to hold them – even quite briefly – in
the centre of our being, which means that once
again the most important thing asked of us is
inner calm and stillness. 'Christ be with *him*;
Christ within *her*.'

But what of all those times when God
seems absent, as he was so often for the Welsh

48

poet-priest R. S. Thomas, as described in his poem *Folk Tale*.

There are, for all of us, many times when prayer is dead, simply an unrewarding slog, when we *feel* nothing and we seem very much alone. The first thing we need to remember is that there is a lot of evidence that in prayer awareness of God is infrequent. A great Benedictine spiritual director, Dom John Chapman, wrote:

> *I fancy that the majority of those religious who practise contemplative prayer would be likely to state that they have no perception whatever of God's presence or of his existence, though they are conscious of an intense desire of him and sometimes an intense love ... They would probably say that they rather want him than perceive him, that they are more conscious of his absence than his presence, and would put down their certainty of him to reason and to faith, more than to perception or consciousness.*

God isn't someone we could experience through our senses if only he were near enough or if only we had a better imagination. He is in fact nearer to us than breathing, 'nearer to me', writes Eckhart, 'than I am to my own self'; and all around are clues to his being. But as the author of *The Cloud of Unknowing* puts it: 'He may well be loved but not thought; by love may he be gotten and holden but by thought never', for thought objectifies and that we cannot do with God. So the heart of prayer is trust: trusting in the God revealed in Christ, and courageously reaching out to him. Thank God when you do have a sense of his reality and his presence, but remember not to confuse *feelings* with *faith*, any more than we should think that we expect to have strong *feelings* in the presence of the one we love most, or doubt that their absence in any way alters the reality of that relationship.

Things buried within

It goes without saying that it is impossible to pray if there is something in our life of which we are ashamed, and which we need to confess. Sometimes such things are obvious: sometimes they go very deep into our unconscious, and they have to be drawn out and faced and memories healed. It's also true that in silence we may find disturbing feelings bubbling up from our unconscious, buried fears and fantasies; and perhaps, in time, that deep anger which is the reverse side of depression. For this exposure of our 'shadow side' is healthy and can be a healing process, though we may need a wise counsellor or spiritual director to help us deal with it. Most of us have had to repress our natural feelings of frustration, anger and resentment at different times of our life – not least in childhood and adolescence – burying them deep rather than expressing them, and then, at moments of real hurt or crisis, such as when a partner dies, the undischarged rage, often rage against God, can emerge. There is a nice poem – *Conversation in Avila* – based on a well-known story about the anger of St Teresa by the American poet Phyllis McGinley.

There is also a lot of anger in the Bible, most of it directed against God. And naturally so. For if God has given us a life that is often manifestly unfair and so full of things that hurt us, is it not natural to rail against him? The psalmist does so, and the prophets, and Job and Jonah. And we should always be honest with God, for what's the point of pretending to be other than we are? If I know myself to be struggling, angry, depressed, tired, then that is what I have to offer to God and I am nonetheless welcomed and nonetheless loved.

When Martin Luther told his confessor that he couldn't pray, he was told it was not because God was angry with him, but because he was angry with God and must learn to tell him so. And

Luther comments: 'This was magnificently said.' So if you want to throw your toys around, throw them at God: he can take it. For ours is a God who doesn't stand apart from our suffering and all our bewildered questions, but in Christ enters into them himself. And on the cross God willingly opens himself to the worst that human anger can do without any diminishing of his love. Indeed at Calvary he invites us to vent our anger upon him in order that we can discover in him a loving forgiveness that overwhelms us.

Do you remember that most *angry* of poems, George Herbert's *The Collar*?

> *I struck the board and cry'd No more.*
> *I will abroad.*
> *What? Shall I ever sigh and pine?*

And the poem, after a torrent of increasingly angry words, ends:

> *But as I rav'd and grew more fierce and*
> *   wilde*
> *At every word,*
> *Me thoughts I heard one calling, Childe:*
> *And I reply'd, My Lord.*

Our Father ...

I have been at pains to stress that prayer is quite simply about the journey inwards: the claiming of a relationship with the Christlike God who if we do not find him within and among us we shall not find at all. 'He is both other than I am', writes Harry Williams, 'and also the same ... The source from which I continually flow. In my deep union with the mystery of another person and in the mystery of my own being, what I find is God.'

And most people find that as they grow older they don't need many prayers, or new techniques, or more books about prayer. We need to use just a few familiar ones more and more deeply: in *public*, the Liturgy and (for some of us) the daily Offices; in *private*, those words from scripture or the psalms or the Jesus prayer or single words; or, perhaps the safest and surest of all, the Lord's Prayer. Not a day has passed in nearly two thousand years when this prayer has not been said, and said in every conceivable situation, by people of all ages and in every nation and in every kind of mood: thankfully, resignedly, thoughtlessly, anxiously, dutifully out of habit, trustingly in pain and in sickness, and at the point of death. 'Lord, teach us to pray', his friends had said to Jesus. And what he does is not simply to tell them *how* to pray but to give them a prayer which will form a bond of unity between them and among all Christians ever after: a kind of signature tune, if you like; all we will ever need to express our trusting relationship with God and our dependence on him.

'Pray like this', he said. Focus your heart and mind and imagination on the Father, who is *our* Father, on the kingdom, on the Father's will, on your daily bread, on the forgiveness of sins and the delivery from evil. Do this, and your bodily and spiritual needs, and those of others, are at once lifted onto a new level: lifted into the orbit of God's will and purpose with the conviction that the kingdom and the glory are his.

That saintly woman, the twentieth-century French philosopher Simone Weil, once wrote:

The Our Father contains all possible petitions ... It is impossible to say it once through, giving the fullest possible attention to every word, without a change, infinitesimal perhaps, but real, taking place in the soul.

And that lovely poet Edwin Muir writes in his autobiography:

Last night, going to bed alone, I suddenly found myself reciting the Lord's Prayer in a loud emphatic voice, with deep urgency and profound and disturbed emotions. While I went on I grew more composed, and gradually my soul grew still; every word had a strange fullness of meaning which astonished and delighted me ... Meaning after meaning sprang from it, overcoming me again with joyful surprise; and I realized that this simple petition was always universal and always inexhaustible... and day by day sanctified human life.

So whether we use the Lord's Prayer, or some other inwardly repeated words, the constant repetition of it, day in and day out, year in and year out, to help us focus down, to lead us into stillness, is not a debasing of the coinage. In fact, quite the reverse. For as the words over the years sink down from the mind into the heart they become the instant means, at any point of the day or night, of recalling the relationship in which we stand with the Christlike God, whose love always exceeds our expectations and our imagining.

3.

Looking to Jesus

I began by saying that whether or not we pray depends on how we conceive of God. I want to end by saying that whether or not we pray also depends in the end on how much we actually *want* to do so. 'Our one desire and choice', writes St Ignatius in his *Spiritual Exercises*, 'should be: what is more conducive to the end for which we are created'. What do we desire? What is it that we really want in this life? A safe and fulfilling job? To win the lottery? An unworrying family life? A comfortable old age with a small garden? Good health? An MBE? Oh, I am not mocking such aims: they are fine in their own way. But what about the pearl of great price, the treasure hidden in a field? What about discovering the relationship that stands firm in the face of every disappointment, every kind of sickness and disaster, even death itself? What about responding to that deepest of all desires – the desire of the creature for his or her creator?

For the treasure hidden in a field of which Jesus speaks is hidden within the field of our own inner life, our divided self, that complex mix of thoughts, memories, emotions, fears and conflicting desires which we only dimly perceive, but which God 'to whom all hearts are open, all desires known' sees utterly clearly. It is our surface desires that are the loudest and most demanding, yet when we answer them we can be left feeling frustrated and unsatisfied.

God's desire is that we shall discover what we really want and who we really are. Yet it is only as we come to see the deep attractiveness of the love of God that we begin to desire him, and then his deepest desire for us, and our deepest desire for us, become one.

So: will the real me please stand up? Stand up and become what I truly am, and take my place among the redeemed and liberated Easter people.

Thomas Merton has a prayer that goes like this:

My Lord God,
I have no idea where I am going.
I do not see the road ahead of me.
I cannot know for certain where it will end.
Nor do I really know myself,
and the fact that I think I am following your
    will does not mean that I am actually
    doing so.
But I believe that the desire to please you
does in fact please you.
And I hope I have that desire in all that I am
    doing.
I hope that I will never do anything apart
    from that desire.
And I know that if I do this you will lead me
    by the right road, though I may know
    nothing about it.
Therefore will I trust you always though I
    may seem lost and in the shadow of death.
I will not fear, for you are ever with me, and
    you will never leave me to face my perils
    alone.

My final concern is that you should be under no illusions about me: that you should understand that those who write books, or preach sermons, or give addresses on prayer, do so because of what they *lack*, not because of what they *have*. I have spoken of what I *long for*, not of what I possess; of how I would *like* to be, not of what I am. Of one who travels with you on the journey, sometimes tentatively, often not very confidently, yet always with hope, 'looking to Jesus, the author and perfecter of our faith'.

Books by Michael Mayne

All available from Darton, Longman and Todd
www.dltbooks.com

The Enduring Melody

'An heroic book. Begun in health as a meditation on a lifetime's faith and experience, it ends in mortal sickness with Michael Mayne facing death. But his courage, his humour and his tone of voice do not desert him; humbling and inspiring, it is a validation both of his faith and his humanity.' Alan Bennett

'An autobiography of dying. It was brave to write it and it needs courage to read it, but the benefits are enormous. Michael Mayne belongs to the great priest-writers. He takes on the issues of mortality, both in religion and literature, and makes us all discover what pain has taught him. It is a wonderful achievement.' Ronald Blythe

ISBN: 978-0-232-52687-5; eBook 978-0-232-52818-3

God's Consoling Love
Sermons and Addresses

This new selection of previously unpublished writing by Michael Mayne has been compiled by Joel Huffstetler, the leading scholar of Mayne's work. Wherever we find ourselves on our spiritual journey, this collection of wise words will help us draw closer to the reality of the self-giving love that lies at the heart of God.

'Michael's ministry ... was a ministry of love ... love poured out abundantly, in a movement and spirit that is

faithful to the example of Jesus Christ. I am grateful to encounter him so powerfully in these sermons, and to explore with him "the secret of the universe revealed in the alphabet of human words and actions, the words and actions of (Jesus Christ), who revealed, both in his life and his death, the breath-taking power of God's mercy and the meaning of unlimited forgiveness".' The Revd Richard Coles

ISBN: 978-0-232-53017-9

Learning to Dance

Few writers have explored the borderland between faith and contemporary living more eloquently and engagingly in recent years than Michael Mayne. In *Learning to Dance* he creates a magical weave of poetry, science and spirituality, touching on the longings, doubts and hopes of all of us.

'A landmark in the exploration of contemporary spirituality ... This is the kind of book - a rare event - that one would happily take away to the mythical desert island.' Margaret Silf

ISBN: 978-0-232-52434-5

Pray, Love, Remember

Michael Mayne examines the meaning of praying, loving and remembering, and their implications for the life of the Church, basing each chapter on the theme of the collects from Ash Wednesday to Easter Day.

'A wonderfully readable mixture. Pray, Love, Remember *is a Lenten book but it is not a dutiful read.'* Alan Bennett

ISBN: 978-0-232-52270-9

Prayer

With great economy and elegance, Michael Mayne, one the greatest spiritual writers of the last century, writes practically, simply, briefly and beautifully about prayer.

Prayer is not primarily something *one does*. Prayer is something *that is*. It is in God that we live and move and have our being. God is always in us, waiting to be released into expression.

ISBN: 978-0-232-53016-2

This Sunrise of Wonder
Letters for the Journey

Michael Mayne's genius was to stir the reader to sit up and *see*, to notice the world as if for the first time. *This Sunrise of Wonder* is a collection of letters written over 20 years ago for his two grandchildren, Adam and Anna, that beautifully and memorably expresses Mayne's vision of life. For him, to be human is to learn to be attentive, to recognise the mystery of people and of things. Learn how to see, he tells us, for to see is the beginning of wonder.

'This is a generous, life-enhancing book, to cherish and to keep.' A. N. Wilson

ISBN: 978-0-232-52742-1

To Trust and to Love
Sermons and Addresses

A wonderful introduction to a collection of Michael Mayne's previously unpublished pieces, sermons and addresses.

With insight and wry humour he shows us how to see the things of God in art and in science, in poetry and in architecture, as well as in the scriptures and in liturgy. He makes the Christian understanding of life intelligible and attractive for people inside and far outside the churches. He teaches us to notice, to wonder, to be astonished. We learn to trust, and to love.

ISBN: 978-0-232-52798-8

A Year Lost and Found

A poignant complement to Michael Mayne's last book, *The Enduring Melody*, which was written twenty years later, in the final months of his life.

'This unashamedly is a very personal book about one year of my life and what a sudden, mysterious, knockdown kind of illness does to you and your family; about doctors and their still limited knowledge in certain areas; and about a God who stops you dead in your tracks and sets you groping for answers.'

'Michael Mayne writes the kind of theology that works for those of us who switch off when we hear yet another dry sermon or turn the pages of one more eminently forgettable book. His theology is carved, often extremely painfully, out of real life, his life, with all the experiences, encounters and exchanges which make his life – and each of our lives – unique.' From the Foreword by Sister Frances Dominica, All Saints Sisters of the Poor

ISBN: 978-0-232-52715-5